SMASHING!

The Chemistry of Atoms

Written by William D. Adams

www.worldbook.com

Co-published by agreement between Shi Tu Hui and World Book, Inc.

Shi Tu Hui
Room 1807, Block 1,
#3 West Dawang Road
Chaoyang District, Beijing 100025
P.R. China

World Book, Inc.
180 North LaSalle Street
Suite 900
Chicago, Illinois 60601
USA

© 2026. All rights reserved. This volume may not be reproduced in whole or in part in any form without prior written permission from the publisher.

WORLD BOOK and the GLOBE DEVICE are registered trademarks or trademarks of World Book, Inc.

Library of Congress Control Number: 2025942234

Aha! Academy: Chemistry
ISBN: 978-0-7166-7346-0 (set, hardcover)

Smashing! The Chemistry of Atoms
ISBN: 978-0-7166-7348-4 (hard cover)
ISBN: 978-0-7166-7368-2 (e-book)
ISBN: 978-0-7166-7358-3 (soft cover)

Staff

Editorial

Vice President
Tom Evans

Senior Manager, New Content
Jeff De La Rosa

Senior Curriculum Designer
Caroline Davidson

Curriculum Designer
Mikayla Kightlinger

Content Creator
Joseph P. Cataliotti

Proofreader
Nathalie Strassheim

Indexer
Nathaniel Lindstrom

Graphics and Design

Senior Visual
Communications Designer
Melanie Bender

Designer
Shannon Hagman

Written by William D. Adams

Designed by Starletta Polster

Acknowledgments

The publishers gratefully acknowledge the following sources for photography. All illustrations were prepared by WORLD BOOK unless otherwise noted.

Cover: 3d_hokage/Shutterstock; curraheeshutter/Shutterstock; Ezume Images/Shutterstock; Mark_Kostich/Shutterstock; Jurik Peter/Shutterstock

© INTERFOTO/Alamy 11, 25; © Photo 12/Alamy 38; © Science History Images/Alamy 7, 17; © Sputnik/AP Photo 19; © Daily Herald Archive/Contributor/Getty Images; Lasunncty (licensed under CC BY-SA 4.0) 21; NASA 31; Public Domain 34; Radiogenic (licensed under CC0 1.0) 29; © Shutterstock 3, 4, 5, 6, 7, 8, 9, 10, 11, 12, 13, 14, 15, 16, 17, 18, 19, 20, 21, 22, 23, 24, 25, 26, 27, 28, 29, 30, 31, 32, 33, 34, 35, 36, 37, 38, 39, 40, 41, 42, 43, 44, 45, 46, 47, 48; © United States Department of Energy

There is a glossary of terms on page 48. Terms defined in the glossary are in type that looks like *this* on their first appearance on any spread (two facing pages).

Contents

Introduction 4

① **Atomic basics** 6
    Anatomy of an atom 8
    The periodic table. 10
    Reading the periodic table 12
    Atomic mass and isotopes. 14

② **Synthetic elements** 16
    Building a bigger atom. 18
    Atomic stability 20
    Vital element: californium 22

③ **Decaying atoms** 24
    Radioactive decay. 26
    Uses of radioactive decay 28

④ **Nuclear fission**. 32
    Vital element: uranium 34
    Uses of fission 36
    Fission problems 38

⑤ **Nuclear fusion**. 40
    Unlimited energy? 42

Visualizing half-life. 44
Index 46
Glossary 48

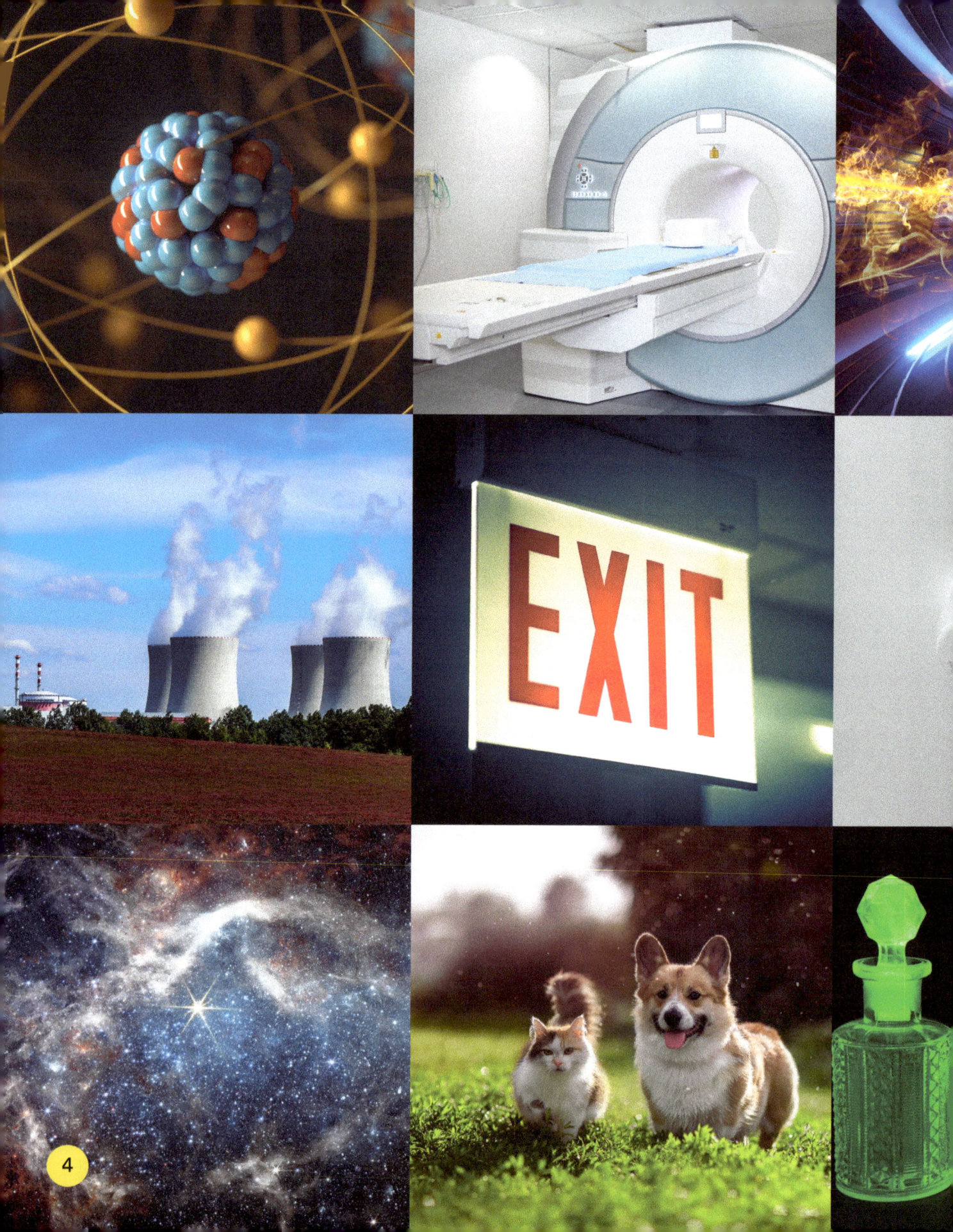

Introduction

This book, the walls, yourself, the air around you—everything is made of atoms. The atom is the basic unit of matter. Atoms come together in chemical reactions to form the molecules and compounds that make up everything in the universe.

You probably knew that already. But did you know that under the right conditions, some atoms can undergo an entirely different series of changes? These changes transform atoms at their most basic level, causing them to defy the rules laid down by traditional chemistry and physics. One atom can turn into two, two atoms can combine into one, one element can turn into another, and energy can be created and destroyed! Read on to learn the fantastic secrets of nuclear chemistry!

Can you guess how much thinner an atom is than a human hair?

1
ATOMIC BASICS

When you think of atoms, you may think of chemical reactions. In such a reaction, atoms of different elements might come together to form a new molecule, for example. Or, a molecule might break apart, releasing energy.

Chemical reactions aren't the only way atoms can power our world, however. The very pieces of atoms themselves can be split up and smashed together, yielding explosive results. To learn more about these processes, we'll first get to know atoms.

From stars to soda pop, atoms are the building blocks out of which all matter is made.

DID YOU KNOW?

An atom is incredibly tiny—more than 1 million times smaller than the thickness of a human hair. The smallest speck that can be seen under an ordinary microscope contains more than 10 billion atoms.

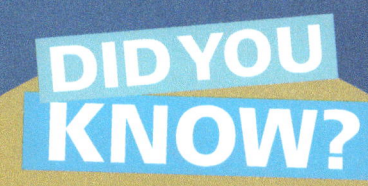

The idea that everything is made up of a few simple parts originated during the 400's B.C. in the philosophy of atomism. Atomism was founded by the Greek philosopher Leucippus, but his disciple **Democritus** developed the idea more fully. Democritus gave his basic particle the name *atom*, which means *uncuttable*. He imagined atoms as small, hard particles, all composed of the same substance but of different sizes and shapes. The details of this hypothesis didn't hold up, but let's cut them some slack—they didn't even have microscopes!

Not too shabby!

Atomic basics

Anatomy of an **atom**

Protons and neutrons are about the same size. They clump together and make up the nucleus of the atom. A proton has a positive electrical charge, whereas a neutron has no charge.

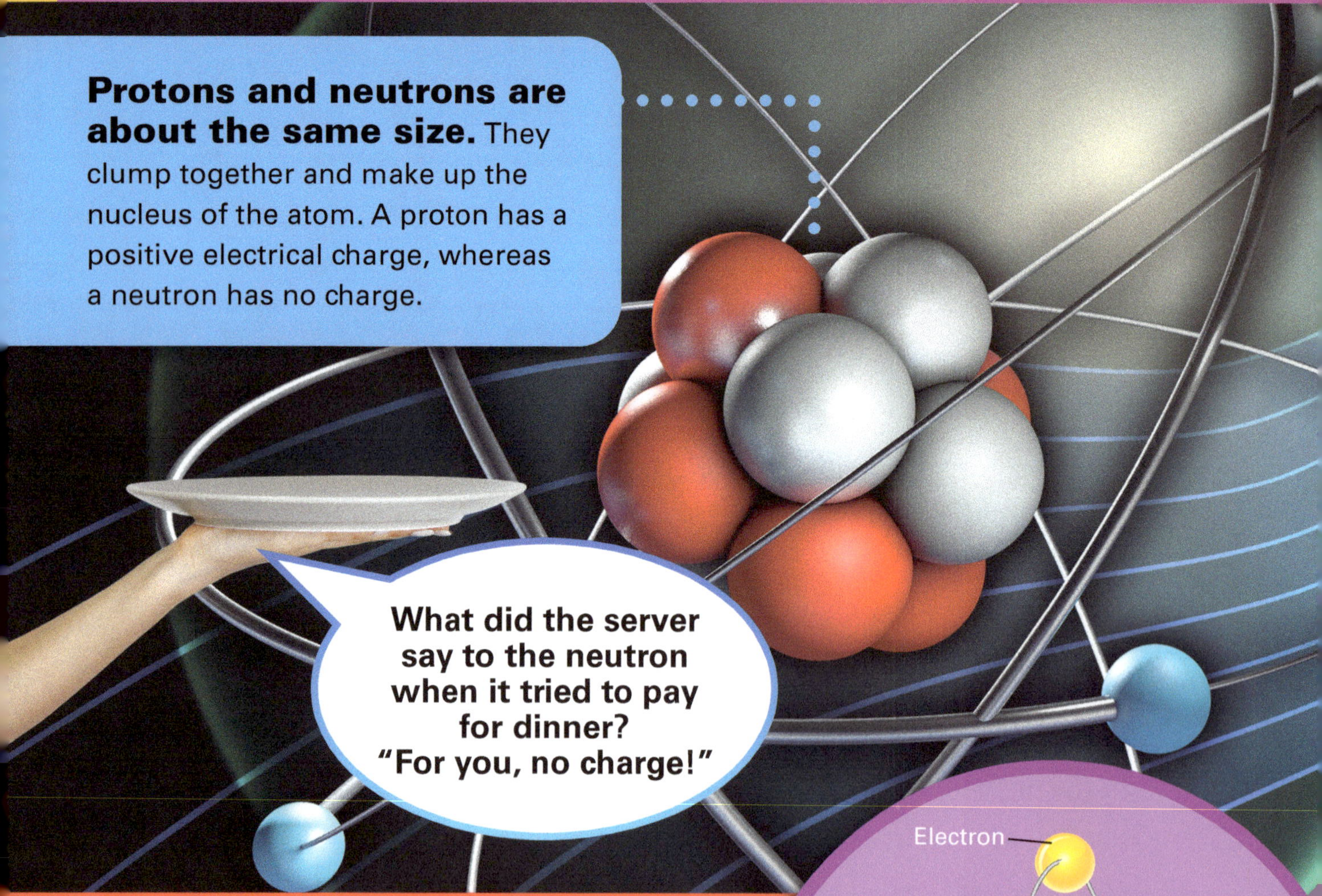

What did the server say to the neutron when it tried to pay for dinner? "For you, no charge!"

Electrons have a negative charge. They are much tinier than protons and neutrons—so tiny that they behave more like waves than particles! Electrons don't stick to the nucleus. Instead, they tend to be found somewhere near it.

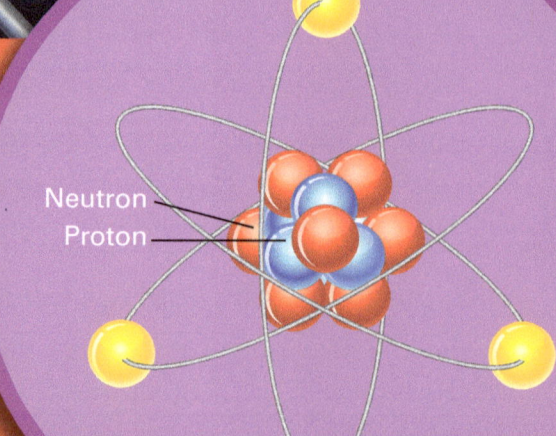

Electron
Neutron
Proton

Atoms may seem impossibly tiny. But, atoms are made up of even smaller parts! Atoms are made of three subatomic particles: protons, neutrons, and electrons.

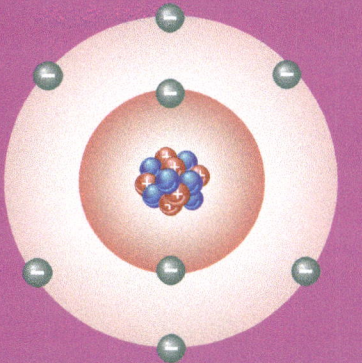

Oxygen atom
- 8 electrons
- 8 protons
- 8 neutrons

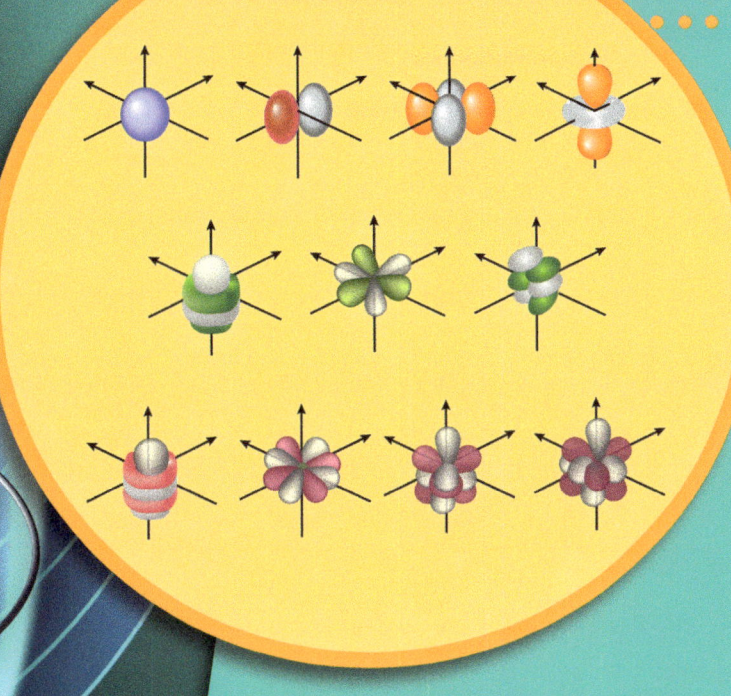

Electrons are usually depicted as tiny spheres orbiting the nucleus in concentric circles, much as moons might orbit a planet. But this simplified view is used for convenience. In truth, electrons are localized in particular regions near the nucleus. These regions, called orbitals, can be different shapes, depending on the type of atom and its energy level. The orbital an electron might be found in depends on how many electrons the atom has and at which energy levels.

Huh, I'm feeling funny. I must have picked up an extra electron.

DID YOU KNOW?

The chemical behavior of an atom is determined largely by the number of electrons in its outermost orbital shell.

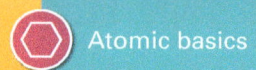 Atomic basics

The periodic table

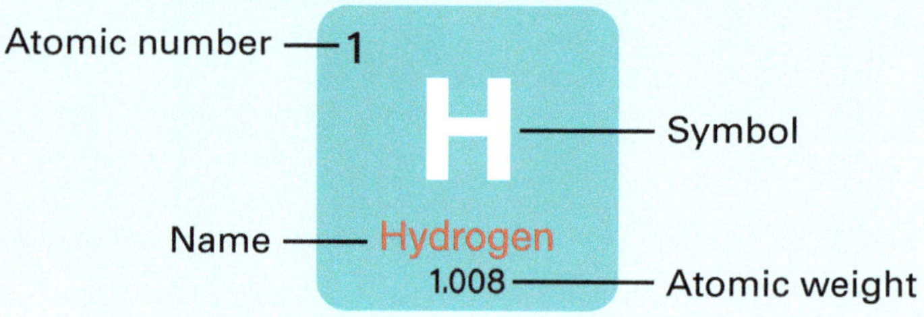

Atomic number — 1
H — Symbol
Name — Hydrogen
1.008 — **Atomic weight**

State of matter (color of name)
GAS LIQUID SOLID UNKNOWN

- Alkali metal
- Lanthanide
- Transition metal
- Alkaline earth metal
- Actinide
- Post-transition metal
- Metalloid
- Polyatomic nonmetal
- Diatomic nonmetal
- Noble gas
- Unknown chemical properties

1 IA	2 IIA	3 IIIB	4 IVB	5 VB	6 VIB	7 VIIB	8 VIIIB	9 VIIIB	10 VIIIB	11 IB	12 IIB
1 **H** Hydrogen 1.008											
3 **Li** Lithium 6.94	4 **Be** Beryllium 9.0121831										
11 **Na** Sodium 22.98976928	12 **Mg** Magnesium 24.305										
19 **K** Potassium 39.0983	20 **Ca** Calcium 40.078	21 **Sc** Scandium 44.955908	22 **Ti** Titanium 47.867	23 **V** Vanadium 50.9415	24 **Cr** Chromium 51.9961	25 **Mn** Manganese 54.938044	26 **Fe** Iron 55.845	27 **Co** Cobalt 58.933194	28 **Ni** Nickel 58.6934	29 **Cu** Copper 63.546	30 **Zn** Zinc 65.38
37 **Rb** Rubidium 85.4678	38 **Sr** Strontium 87.62	39 **Y** Yttrium 88.90584	40 **Zr** Zirconium 91.224	41 **Nb** Niobium 92.90637	42 **Mo** Molybdenum 95.95	43 **Tc** Technetium (98)	44 **Ru** Ruthenium 101.07	45 **Rh** Rhodium 102.90550	46 **Pd** Palladium 106.42	47 **Ag** Silver 107.8682	48 **Cd** Cadmium 112.414
55 **Cs** Caesium 132.90545196	56 **Ba** Barium 137.327	57 – 71 Lanthanoids	72 **Hf** Hafnium 178.49	73 **Ta** Tantalum 180.94788	74 **W** Tungsten 183.84	75 **Re** Rhenium 186.207	76 **Os** Osmium 190.23	77 **Ir** Iridium 192.217	78 **Pt** Platinum 195.084	79 **Au** Gold 196.966569	80 **Hg** Mercury 200.592
87 **Fr** Francium (223)	88 **Ra** Radium (226)	89 – 103 Actinoids	104 **Rf** Rutherfordium (267)	105 **Db** Dubnium (268)	106 **Sg** Seaborgium (269)	107 **Bh** Bohrium (270)	108 **Hs** Hassium (269)	109 **Mt** Meitnerium (278)	110 **Ds** Darmstadtium (281)	111 **Rg** Roentgenium (282)	112 **Cn** Copernicium (285)

57 **La** Lanthanum 138.90547	58 **Ce** Cerium 140.116	59 **Pr** Praseodymium 140.90766	60 **Nd** Neodymium 144.242	61 **Pm** Promethium (145)	62 **Sm** Samarium 150.36	63 **Eu** Europium 151.964	64 **Gd** Gadolinium 157.25	65 **Tb** Terbium 158.92535	66 **Dy** Dysprosium 162.500
89 **Ac** Actinium (227)	90 **Th** Thorium 232.0377	91 **Pa** Protactinium 231.03588	92 **U** Uranium 238.02891	93 **Np** Neptunium (237)	94 **Pu** Plutonium (244)	95 **Am** Americium (243)	96 **Cm** Curium (247)	97 **Bk** Berkelium (247)	98 **Cf** Californium (251)

There are different kinds of atoms— dozens of kinds, in fact. Chemists organize them into a special chart called the periodic table.

The Russian chemist **Dmitri Mendeleev** developed a form of the *periodic law*, the organizing principle behind the periodic table. His law states the properties of chemical elements recur in regular patterns when the elements are arranged according to their mass. Mendeleev created his first chart in 1869. He left blank spaces where he thought there might be undiscovered elements! Later chemists discovered these elements, confirming his predictions.

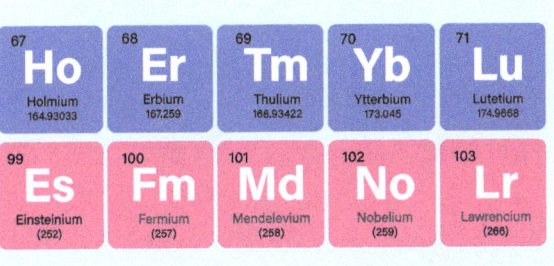

Elements were un-chart-ed territory.

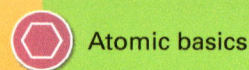 Atomic basics

Reading the periodic table

A chemical symbol is like an element's nickname! Would you rather write out "praseodymium" every time you refer to Element 59 or just "Pr"? Some of the symbols don't match up with the name because they come from another language. Lead, for example, gets the symbol *Pb* from its old Latin name, *plumbum*.

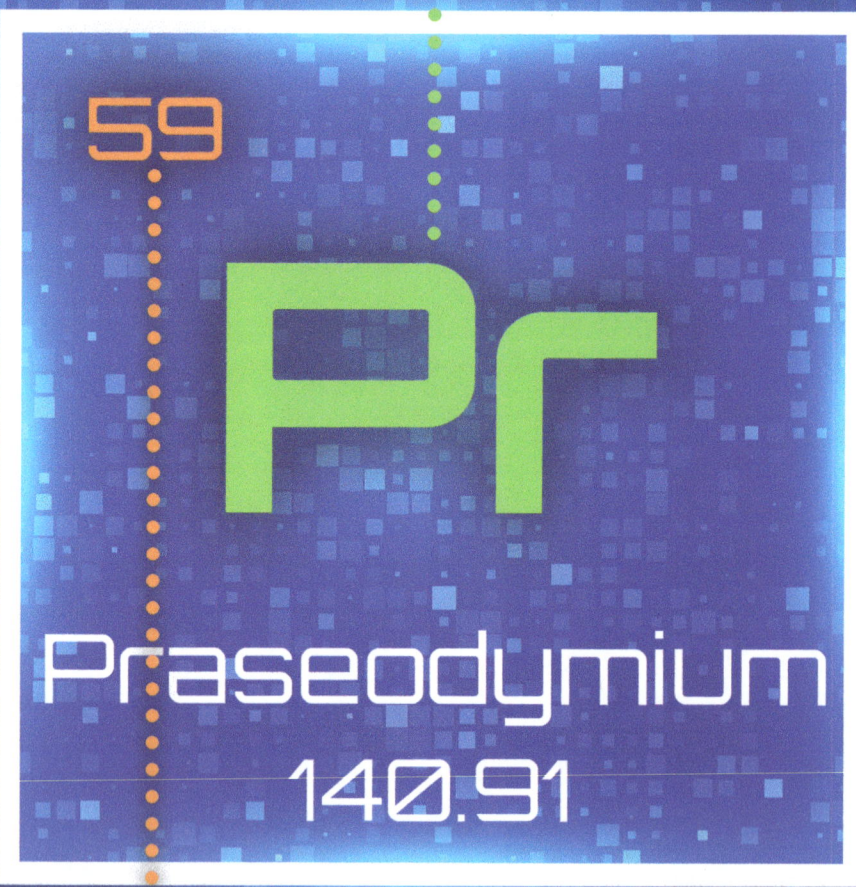

An element is defined by the number of protons it has. Atoms gain and lose electrons all the time, and the number of neutrons can be a bit flexible. But, an atom with one proton is always hydrogen, an atom with two protons is always helium, and so on. The number of protons is so important that chemists call it an element's *atomic number*.

It may seem like the periodic table is written in another language. But once you understand it, you'll find that it's full of useful information about the various kinds of atoms—called chemical elements!

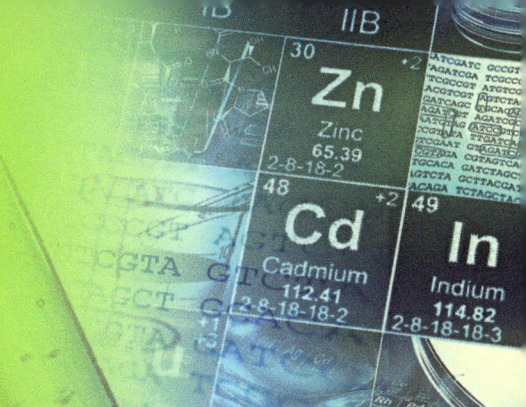

The horizontal rows on the periodic table are called periods. The vertical rows are called groups or families. The elements at the bottom of the chart, the lanthanide and actinide series, belong to no formal family.

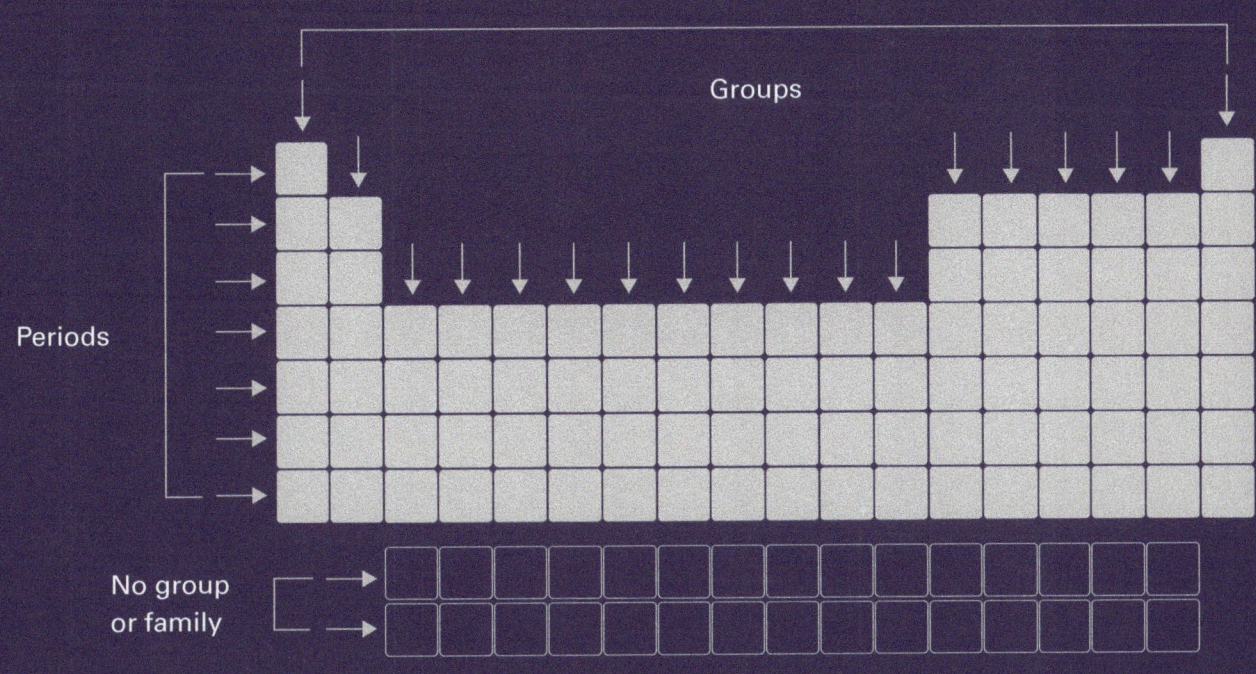

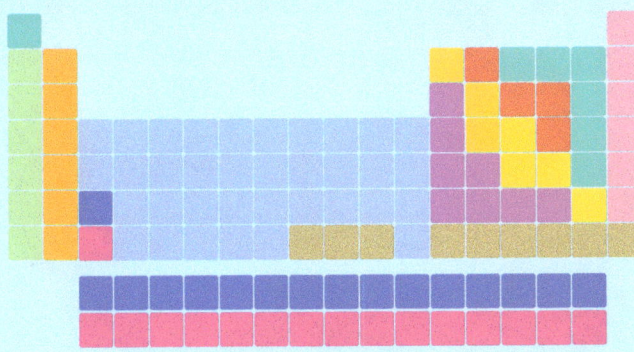

Aside from the period and family, elements often share similar properties with some of their neighbors. Chemists divide the elements into 10 major classes. They are usually denoted on the periodic table by different colors.

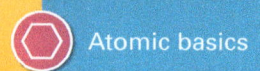
Atomic basics

Atomic mass and isotopes

Calculating atomic mass is easy... Electrons are practically massless, so the only things that count are protons and neutrons. And they're practically the same mass, so it's just a matter of adding up an atom's protons and neutrons to get its atomic mass. Easy!

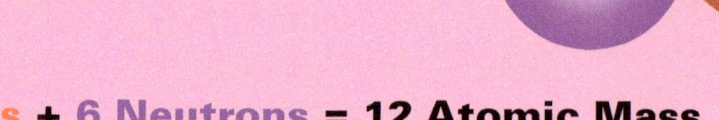
6 Protons + 6 Neutrons = 12 Atomic Mass

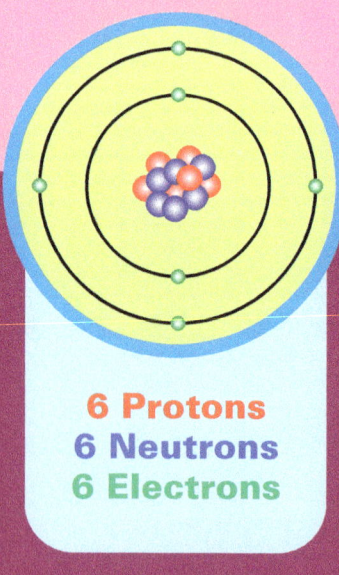

6 Protons
6 Neutrons
6 Electrons

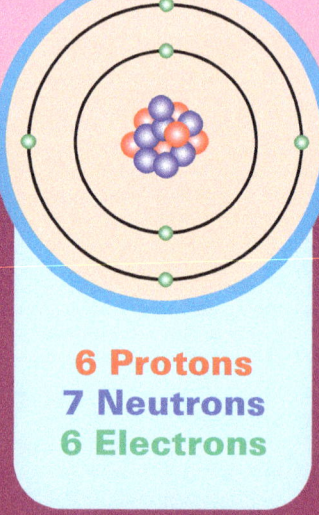

6 Protons
7 Neutrons
6 Electrons

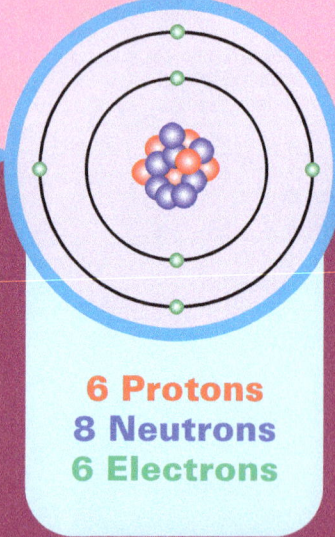

6 Protons
8 Neutrons
6 Electrons

...except it's not quite that easy. Atoms of the same element can have different numbers of neutrons. Such variant atoms are called *isotopes.* Isotopes differ in their abundance—atomic forces make some isotopes easier to form, and others may be slightly unstable and decay (break apart).

How much does an atom weigh?

It's helpful to have a number showing the relative masses of each of the elements. Scientists call this number *atomic mass*.

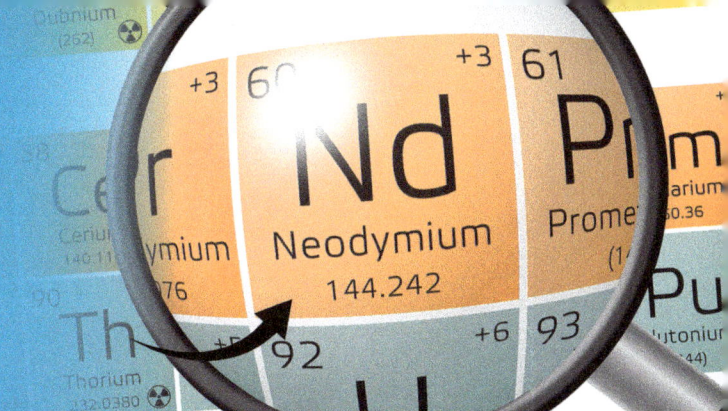

- The good news is that almost any sample of a pure element has the same mix of isotopes. So, chemists use an average of the abundance of the naturally occurring isotopes to come up with the atomic mass. That's why most of the masses have decimals.

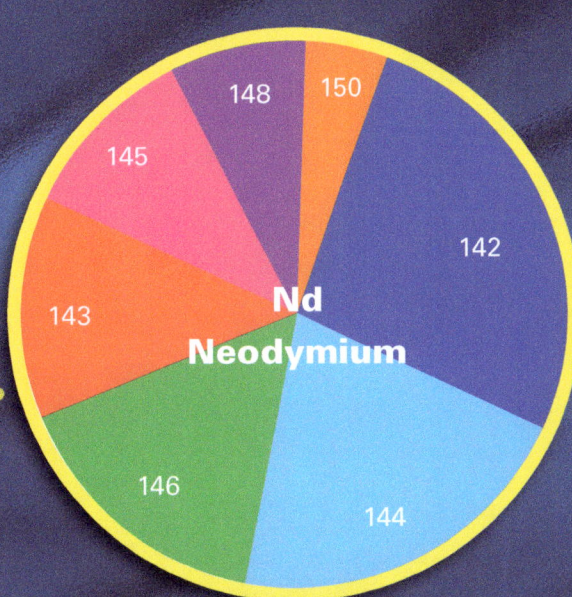

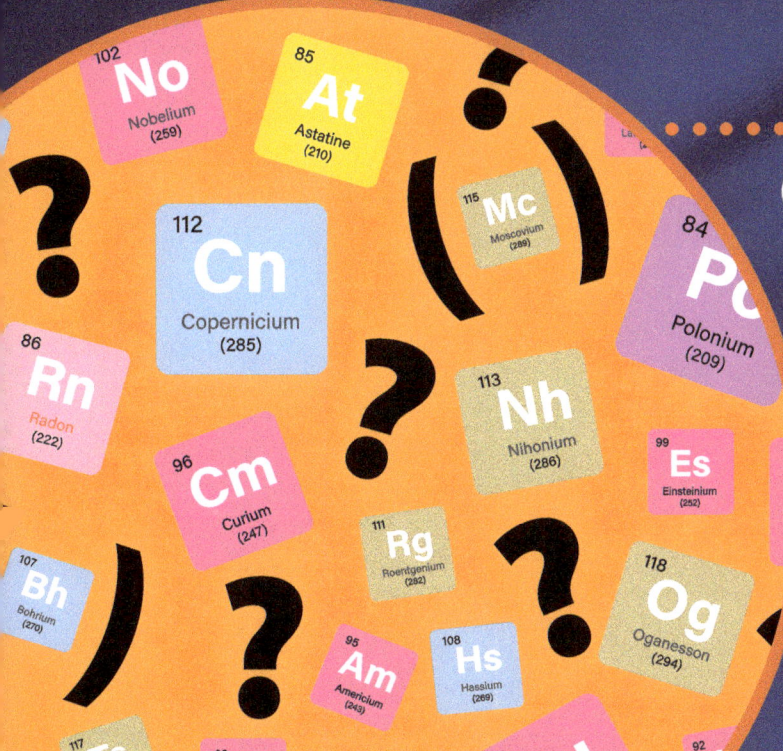

(Close enough.) What about the masses in brackets? These are elements for which no stable isotopes exist in nature. The number in the parentheses or brackets represents the mass of the least unstable isotope.

SYNTHETIC ELEMENTS

Some of the elements on the periodic table are awfully hard to find in the world. In fact, some can't be found outside the lab! Of the 118 elements, about 30 cannot be found in nature. Scientists have been able to create these elements in special laboratory experiments.

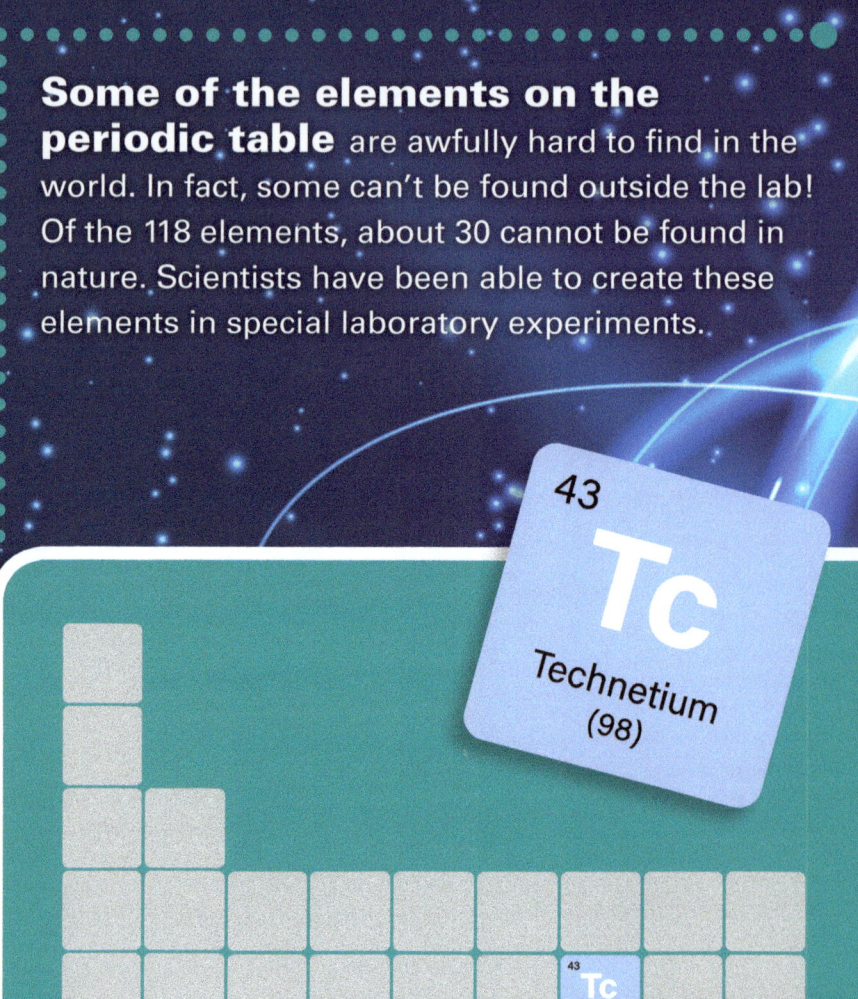

What if you smashed two atomic nuclei together? Would you get a bigger atom? You could! Elements made in this way are called *synthetic elements*. Chemists create them to study the nature of matter.

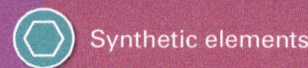
Synthetic elements

Building a bigger atom

The positive charges of protons tend to repel one another. How do they stay together in the nucleus and not fly away? Protons (and neutrons) are attracted to one another by the *strong nuclear force,* one of the most basic forces in the universe. This force acts only at miniscule distances, however, so protons must be very close together for it to take effect.

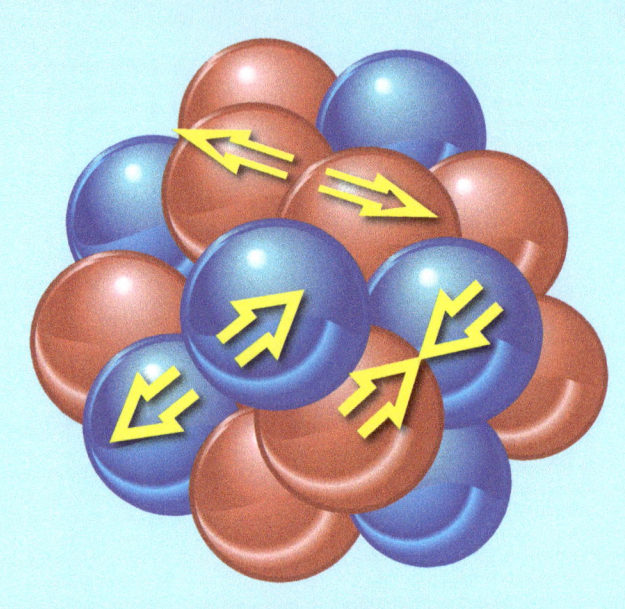

Combining nuclei is harder than just bumping a couple of atoms together. The strong nuclear force holds nuclei together. But something called the *electromagnetic force* keeps atomic nuclei from getting too close to one another.

How do chemists overcome the electromagnetic force? Speed. They fire one atomic nucleus at another one fast enough to overcome the electromagnetic force keeping them apart.

The weird subatomic world is very different from the much larger-scale world in which we live. But, atoms follow the old saw that opposites attract—and likes repel.

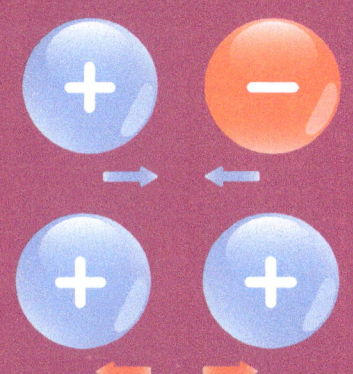

The laboratories that create *synthetic elements* are chock-full of complex equipment and machinery. They're atom factories! Here's just a peek inside an atom builder!

DID YOU KNOW?

Yuri Oganessian is a huge name in atomic research. So huge, in fact, that it's on the periodic table! Oganesson, element 118, was named in honor of the Russian physicist. Oganessian's methods have been used to create many superheavy synthetic atoms.

This is heavy stuff!

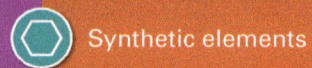 Synthetic elements

Atomic stability

How long does it take for an *isotope* to decay? It's impossible to know for any one atom. Scientists can, however, measure the isotope in bulk and see how long it takes for half of the substance to decay. This amount of time is known as the material's *half-life*.

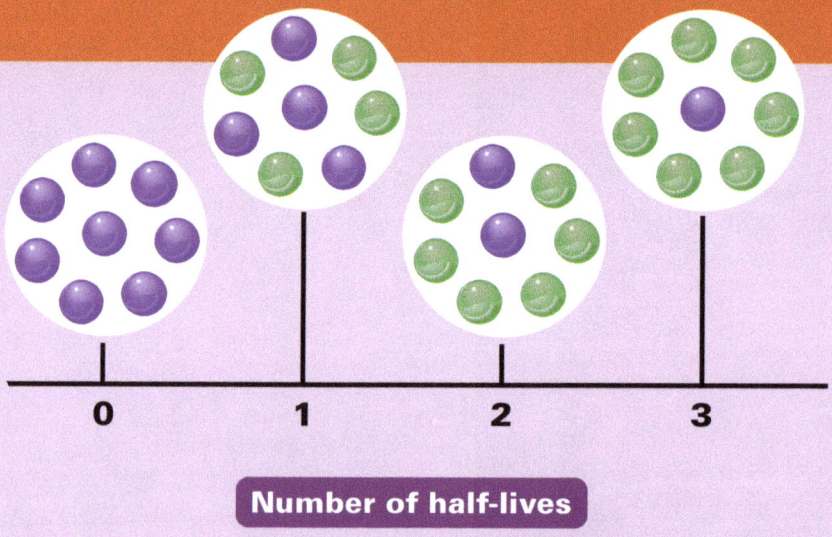

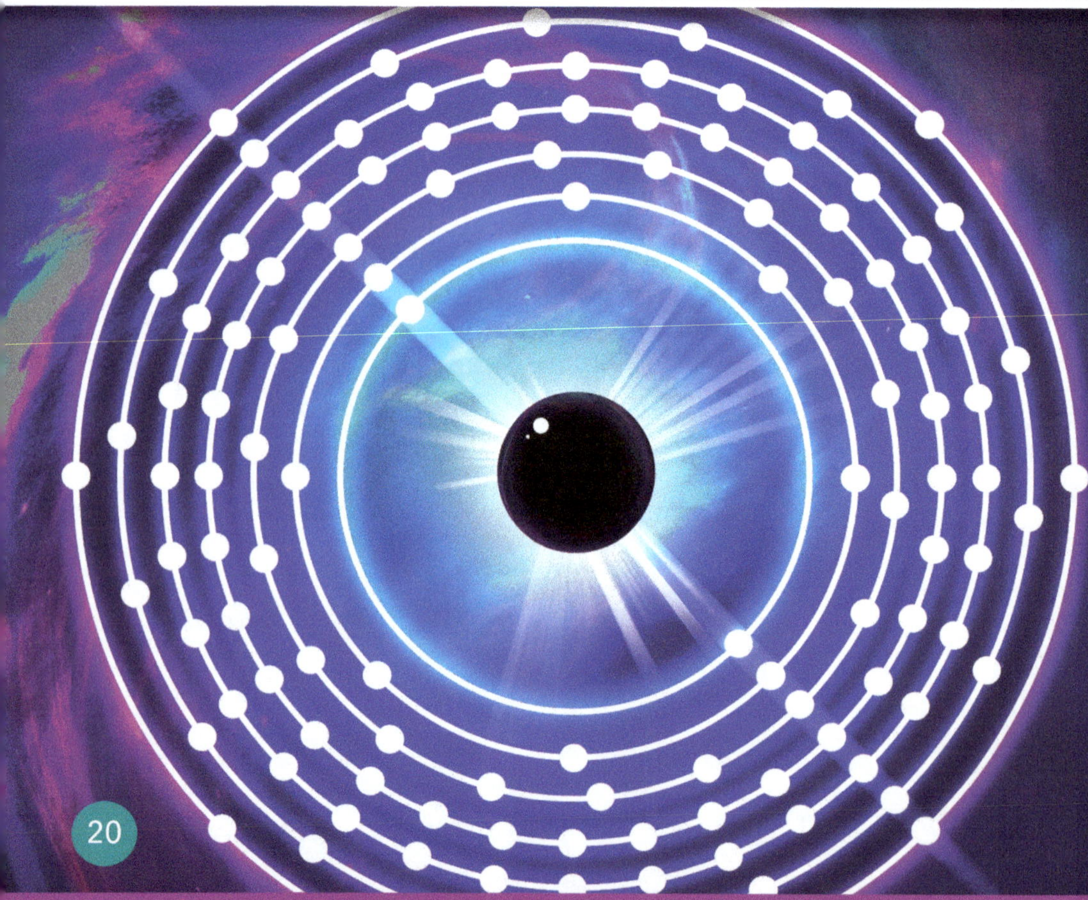

Number of half-lives

Synthetic atoms are unstable, but some last longer than others. Neptunium has a half-life of over 2 million years! That's practically forever in terms of a human lifespan. Oganesson, the largest element created so far, has a half-life of less than 1 millisecond. Blink, and it's gone!

Some isotopes of certain atoms are unstable—particularly synthetic atoms. Eventually, the nucleus will emit a form of *radiation* or split, forming other atoms.

Could we make new stable elements? Researchers can predict approximately how long atomic nuclei will last based on the properties of protons and neutrons and on data gathered from other atoms, arranging these stabilities on a chart. The farther synthetic elements go, the less stable they tend to become. Far out on the chart, however, there's a place where half-lives are predicted to climb back to minutes, hours, and days. Researchers call this region the "island of stability." With large enough *synthetic elements*, we might be able to reach those sparkling shores!

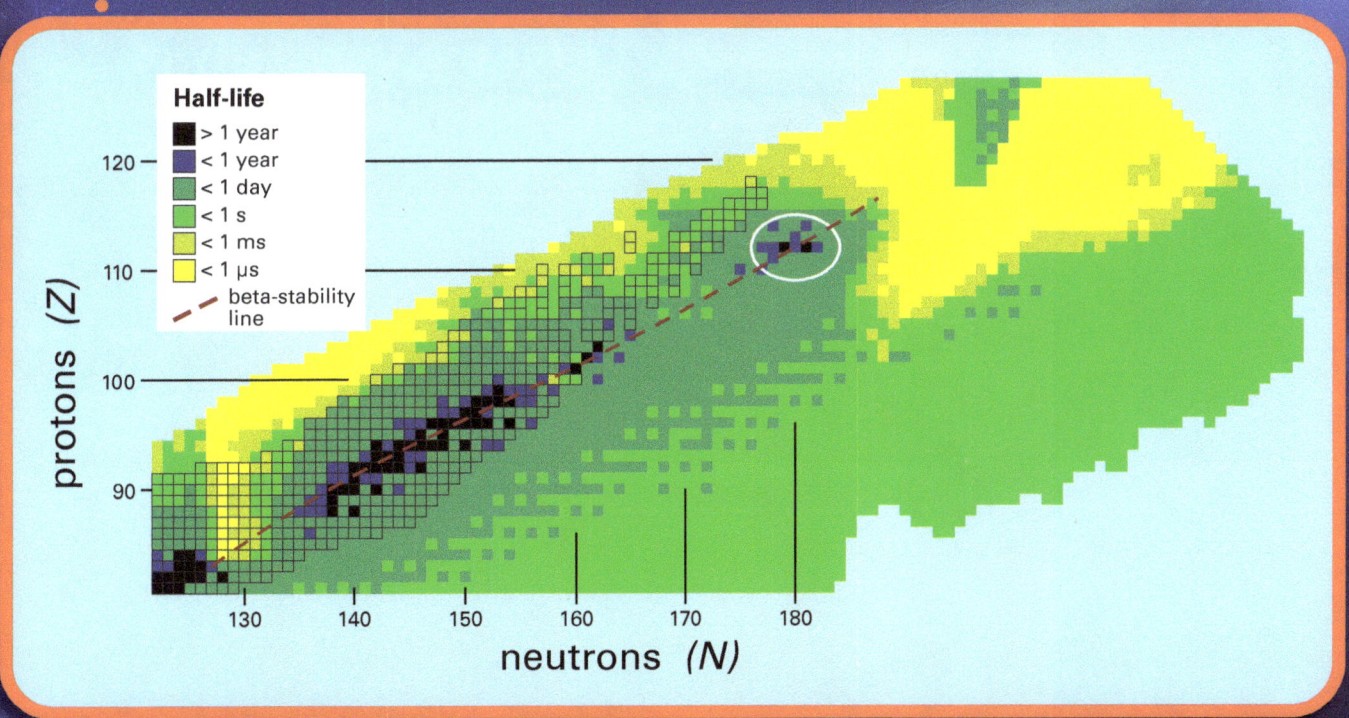

Synthetic elements

Vital element: californium

STATS

Symbol
Cf

Atomic Number
98

Atomic Mass
[251]

Class
Actinides

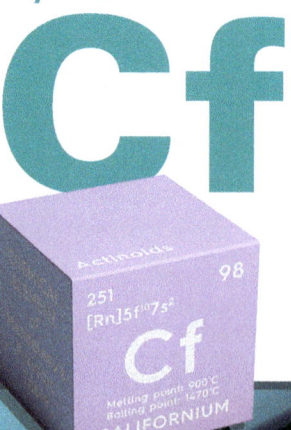

Californium was named for the University of California at Berkeley, where it was discovered in 1950. Scientists there first produced californium by bombarding the element curium with helium ions.

Californium is radioactive—that is, it is an unstable atom that decays to give off radiation. It has a half-life of about 898 years.

Neutron emitter, building block of mega-atoms, extremely harmful if swallowed. Let's explore an important *synthetic element*—californium!

The isotope californium 252 emits lots of neutrons. These neutrons can bounce off such things as underground metal ores, water, and oil. People like those things, so they take portable C-252 emitters into the field to help find them. Californium can also be used to find stress fractures in metal structures or faults in welds.

This should go without saying, but don't handle—and especially, don't eat—any metal of unknown composition! Californium has no biological uses and causes immediate and long-term tissue damage if ingested.

Californium has another use—its large atomic mass and relatively long half-life make it an essential block for building bigger elements. Many of the elements at the bottom of the periodic table have been made by bombarding californium with atoms of another element.

3 DECAYING ATOMS

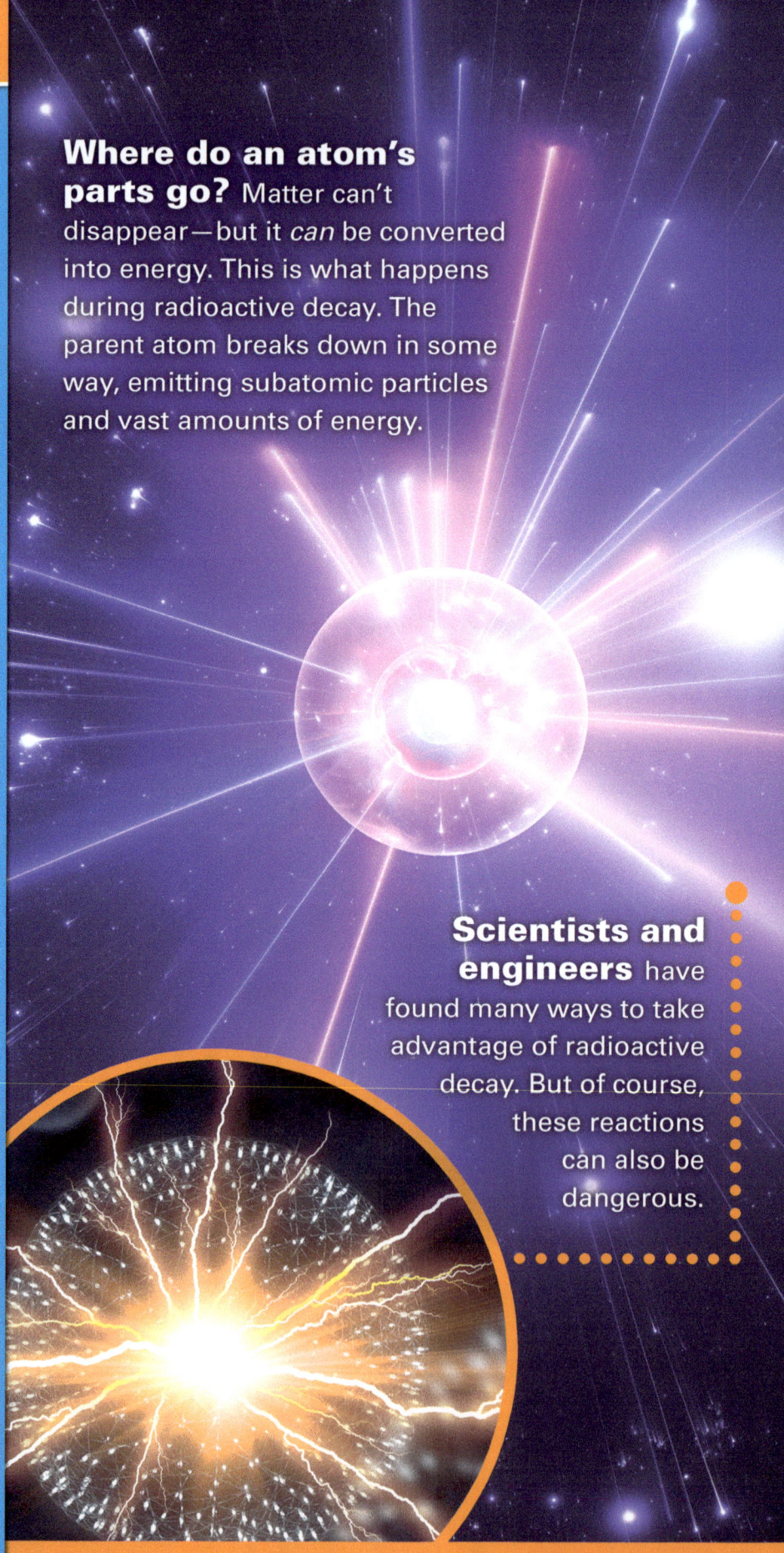

Where do an atom's parts go? Matter can't disappear—but it *can* be converted into energy. This is what happens during radioactive decay. The parent atom breaks down in some way, emitting subatomic particles and vast amounts of energy.

Scientists and engineers have found many ways to take advantage of radioactive decay. But of course, these reactions can also be dangerous.

We've learned that some elements or *isotopes* are **unstable** and will eventually break down. In fact, the heaviest *synthetic elements* only last a small fraction of a second! The breakdown of these atoms is called *radioactive decay*. What happens during this breakdown?

You've heard of $E=mc^2$, right? This is what it's about! The equation says that an object's energy, E, equals the object's mass, m, times the speed of light, c, squared (multiplied by itself). The speed of light is so high that the conversion of a tiny quantity of mass releases a tremendous amount of energy. The physicist **Albert Einstein** came up with this equation in 1905.

Decaying atoms

Radioactive decay

Alpha Decay

Alpha decay occurs when a nucleus spits out an alpha particle. It's just a fancy name for a helium nucleus! It has two protons and two neutrons. Alpha radiation is generally not dangerous. The big particle can't penetrate the skin to affect the bodies of living things.

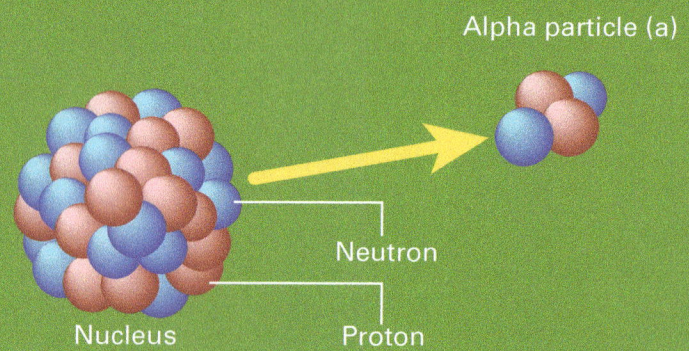

Beta Decay

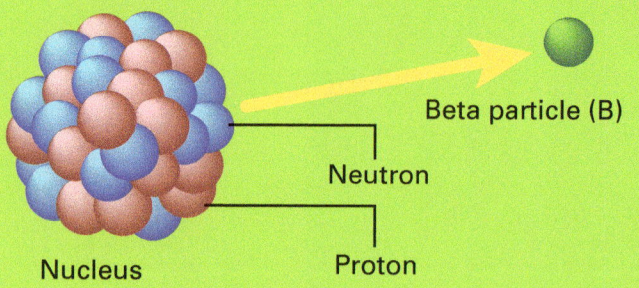

Beta decay occurs when an atom emits either an electron or another subatomic particle called a positron. These particles, collectively called beta particles, can penetrate farther than alpha particles. They can cause burns to exposed skin, but usually clothes are enough to stop them.

Different decaying *isotopes* release different particles. There are three main kinds of *radioactive decay*—known by the Greek letters alpha, beta, and gamma.

Gamma Decay

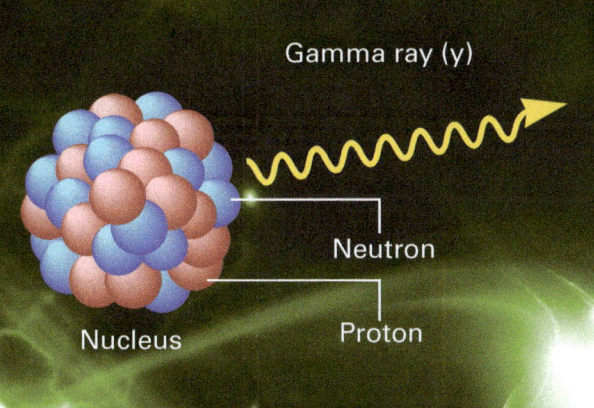

Gamma decay, in which an atom releases gamma waves, usually occurs along with the other two kinds of decay. Gamma rays are extremely dangerous. They can penetrate almost anything and damage cells.

Around 1900, watchmakers mass-produced watches with glow-in-the-dark numbers and hands, made possible through the use of radium-based paint. The element radium emits alpha, beta, and gamma radiation. The companies hired young women to paint the dials and instructed them to shape their brushes to a fine point using their mouths. Scientists and executives knew the radium paint was dangerous, but hid the dangers from their employees. Most of these **"radium girls"** got sick, and many died from radium poisoning over the course of a few years.

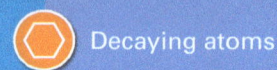

Decaying atoms

Uses of radioactive decay

Many household smoke detectors contain a small amount of the radioactive *isotope* americium 241. This isotope emits alpha particles, which are just helium nuclei. The helium nuclei crave electrons, so they pilfer them from molecules in the air inside the device. A detector senses these ionized air molecules. However, the alpha particles can't ionize smoke. When the detector notices a reduced level of ionization, therefore, it sounds the alarm.

Radioactive decay sounds dangerous, right? In many cases, it is. But believe it or not, products that make use of radioactive decay keep us safe and healthy when used correctly!

Small amounts of radioactive material are used in emergency exit lights. They can show people the way out of buildings or airplanes even when the power is out. It's different than everyday glow-in-the-dark materials—these signs glow even without exposure to light from another source.

CURIOUS CONNECTIONS

RADIOMETRIC DATING

The discovery of radiation greatly helped two unlikely fields: archaeology and paleontology. Small quantities of radioactive isotopes exist naturally in the environment. Living things absorb them as they grow. When they die, their uptake of these isotopes stops. Scientists know how much of these isotopes are in the environment and what their half-lives are. Therefore, they can often determine the age of a fossil or other artifact based on the amount of a particular isotope it has left.

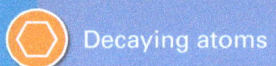

Uses of radioactive decay (continued)

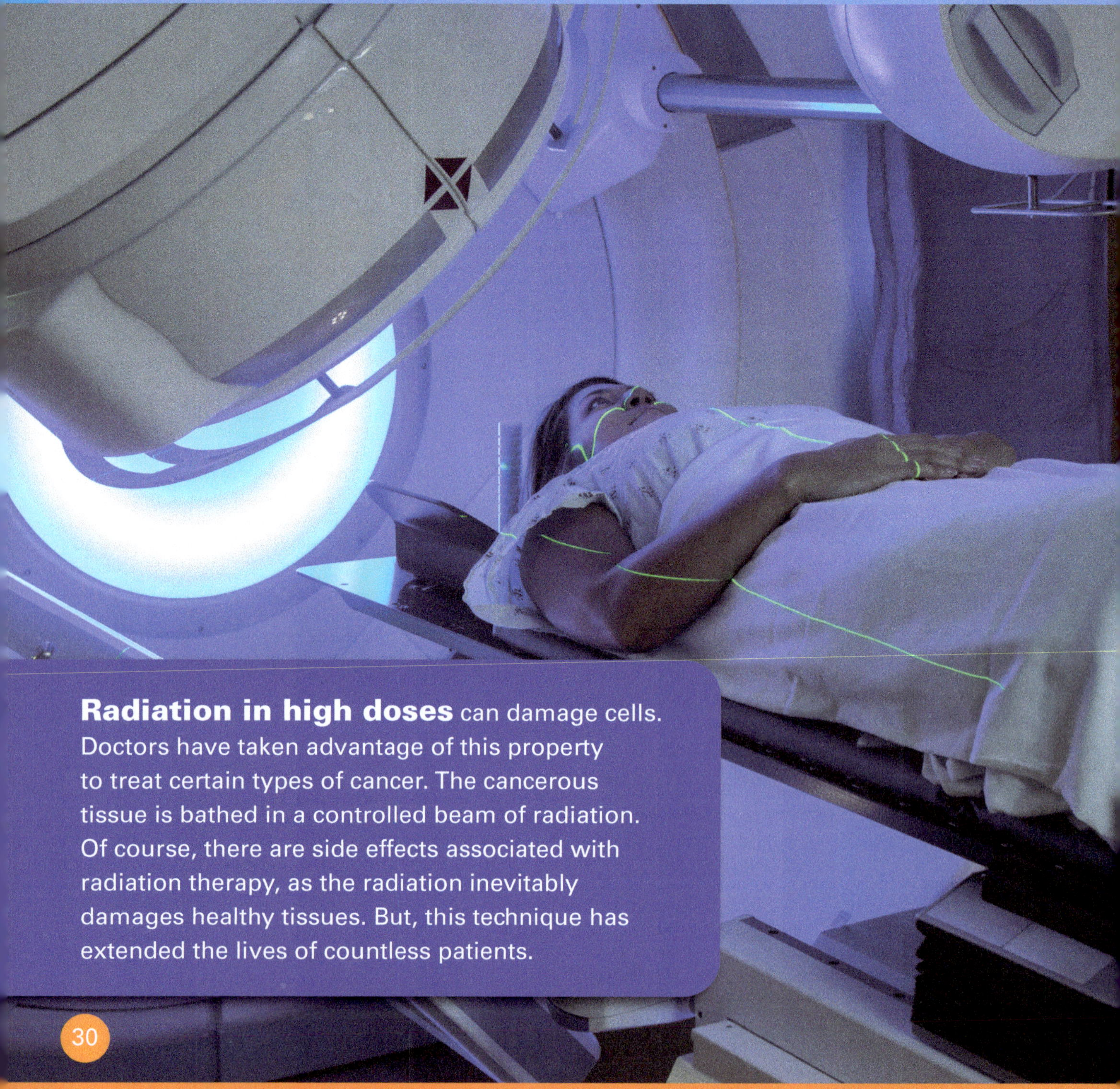

Radiation in high doses can damage cells. Doctors have taken advantage of this property to treat certain types of cancer. The cancerous tissue is bathed in a controlled beam of radiation. Of course, there are side effects associated with radiation therapy, as the radiation inevitably damages healthy tissues. But, this technique has extended the lives of countless patients.

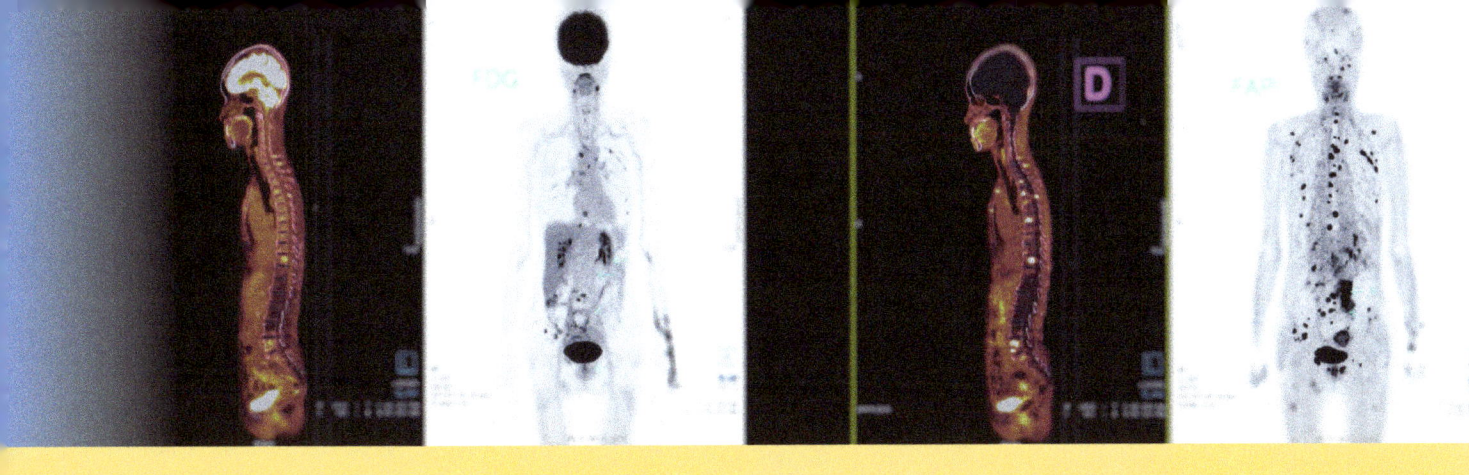

Certain radioactive chemicals can help doctors identify and study damaged or diseased tissue. When taken by mouth or injected, these chemicals get taken up more easily by certain body parts, such as damaged heart tissue. Doctors can then study the area by observing the emitted radiation.

TECH TIME

Devices called radioisotope thermo-electric generators (RTG's) are like nuclear batteries! They convert heat from decaying *isotopes* directly into electricity. It's not a very efficient conversion, but an RTG needs no moving parts. It is thus a useful power source in places where refueling or repair is impossible. One of those places is space! In the inner solar system, probes and rovers are often designed to use solar power. But farther from the sun, many rely on RTG's to stay powered for years—or even decades!

NUCLEAR FISSION

Uranium is a classic example of *radioactive decay*. It splits into two other atoms. Along with these "daughter atoms," the reaction produces lots of energy, all three types of radiation, and a free neutron. One isotope of uranium, U-235, splits when it is hit by a neutron. Therefore, U-235 can start a chain reaction, where one decay releases a neutron that initiates the next decay and so on. Such a chain reaction is called *nuclear fission*.

Atom may mean uncuttable in Greek, but in fact, an atom can be divided. As atomic *isotopes* decay into other isotopes, sometimes they split into two new atoms.

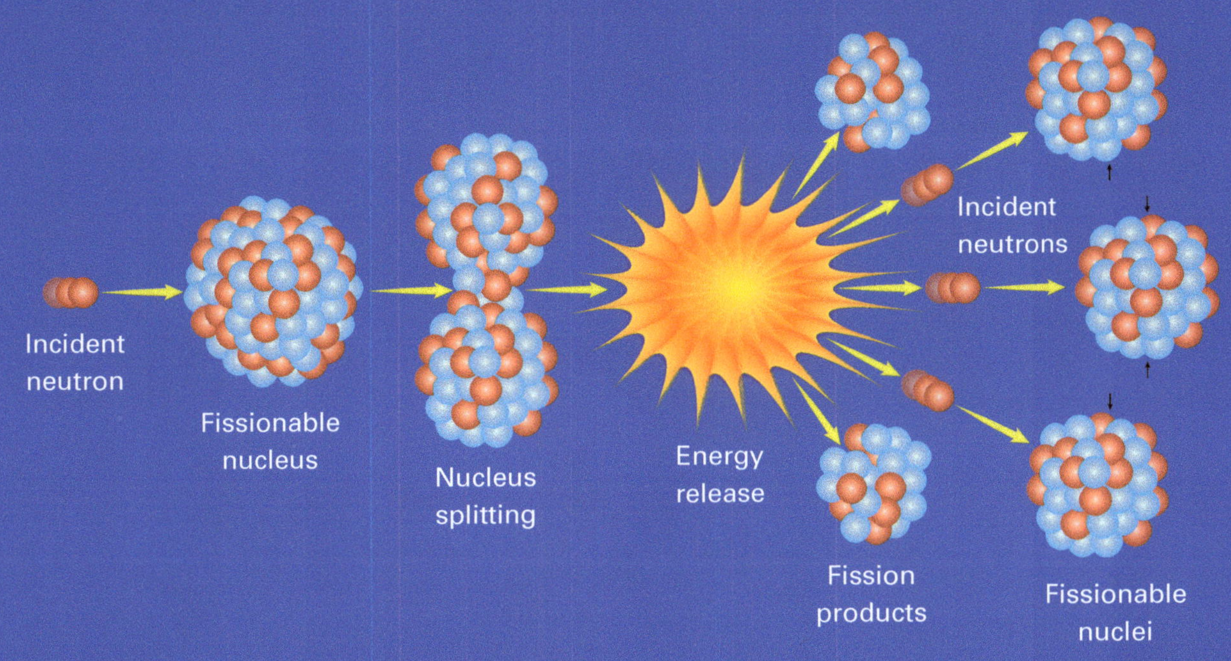

Incident neutron → Fissionable nucleus → Nucleus splitting → Energy release → Fission products, Incident neutrons, Fissionable nuclei

Fission releases an enormous amount of energy.
It can be used for many purposes—some constructive, some destructive.

33

 Nuclear fission

Vital element: uranium

STATS

Symbol
U

Atomic Number
92

Atomic Mass
238.02891

Class
Actinides

"A new element for a new planet!"

In 1789, the German chemist **Martin H. Klaproth** discovered uranium in a mineral called pitchblende. Klaproth named uranium after the planet Uranus, which had been discovered in 1781. In 1841, French chemist Eugène Péligot separated pure uranium from pitchblende.

DID YOU KNOW?

Uranium is heavy! It has a density of 19.1 grams per cubic centimeter. That's even denser than lead!

Uranium is one of the densest materials in the world. Rock deposits throughout the world contain uranium.

Uranium is a glowing example

of *nuclear fission*. But, that's not the only thing it can do. Read on to find out more about this radioactive resource!

Because it is so dense, uranium is used as trim ballast in airplane parts (added weight to make the plane more stable in flight), for armor-piercing shells, and armor for vehicles. Uranium is also used to make decorative glass that *fluoresces* (glows) when exposed to ultraviolet light. Groovy!

Is it safe? A lump of pure uranium gives off fewer gamma rays than a lump of granite! In fact, because it's so dense, uranium is used as a radiation shield in medical imaging devices and in the storage of radioactive materials. Only U-235 is dangerous when separated from other *isotopes*.

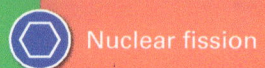
Nuclear fission

Uses of fission

Fission can be used to produce electric power in a nuclear reactor. A nuclear reactor makes use of specially designed uranium fuel pellets enriched with higher than normal levels of U-235. When brought close together, these fuel pellets reach *criticality*, meaning they produce enough neutrons to sustain a chain reaction but no more. These red-hot fuel pellets are stacked in rods and heat a surrounding fluid to high temperatures. The heated fluid turns water into steam, which drives a turbine, generating electric power.

Nuclear fission can generate a lot of power. That power can be used constructively or destructively.

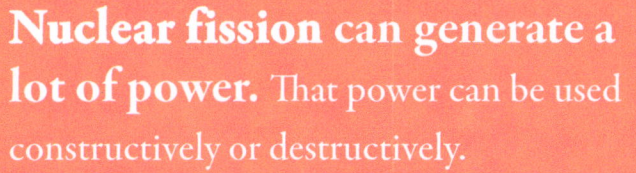

Of course, all that power can also be used for destruction. If U-235 or other fissionable ions are concentrated together, they can reach *supercriticality*. Supercriticality is when the fission reaction is producing more neutrons than needed to sustain a steady chain reaction. Instead, fission occurs rapidly and produces a colossal explosion. Military scientists have used this property to create devastating nuclear weapons.

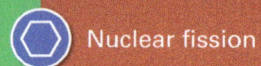

Nuclear fission

Fission **problems**

Would you want nuclear waste stored in your neighborhood? Eventually, nuclear fuel pellets decay to the point that they can't be used for power anymore. Spent nuclear fuel is still radioactive and highly toxic, and it will stay that way for thousands of years. Yikes! How can you keep something safe for so long? Scientists, engineers, and policymakers have tried for decades to figure out how and where to store spent nuclear fuel in the United States, but it all still sits in temporary storage at nuclear power plants.

By their nature, nuclear reactors are always hot. There are ways to control the heat, but if these fail, the core can melt. The fuel mixes with melted control rods and structural materials to form lavalike "corium." Such a nuclear meltdown can spread radioactive material into the air or water.

Fission technology involves extreme temperatures and dangerous radiation. So when things go wrong, they go really wrong!

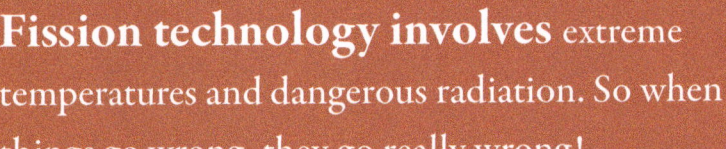

Nuclear weapons are so powerful that they have the potential to wipe out human life. No country has used them since the end of World War II in 1945. But policymakers worry that a terrorist attack, escalating tensions, or even just a misunderstanding could trigger a catastrophic nuclear war.

On April 26, 1986, a nuclear meltdown occurred at the **Chernobyl** power plant, in what is now Ukraine, claiming at least 31 lives. The release of radioactive materials forced the nearby towns of Chernobyl and Prypyat (now Chornobyl and Prypiat) to be evacuated. Prypiat was permanently abandoned.

NUCLEAR FUSION

Nuclear fusion powers the stars. Smaller stars combine hydrogen to form helium. Larger stars fuse hydrogen as well as heavier elements. The enormous amount of energy released prevents the star from collapsing in on itself under its own gravitation. It also shines out as light. It's often said that we are all stardust, because the elements carbon, oxygen, and nitrogen that make up organic molecules were all produced through fusion in the cores of stars.

If atoms can be split through *nuclear fission*, can they be combined? Yes! This process, called *nuclear fusion*, fuses (combines) two or more atomic nuclei into a larger nucleus. Nuclear fusion can also release huge amounts of energy.

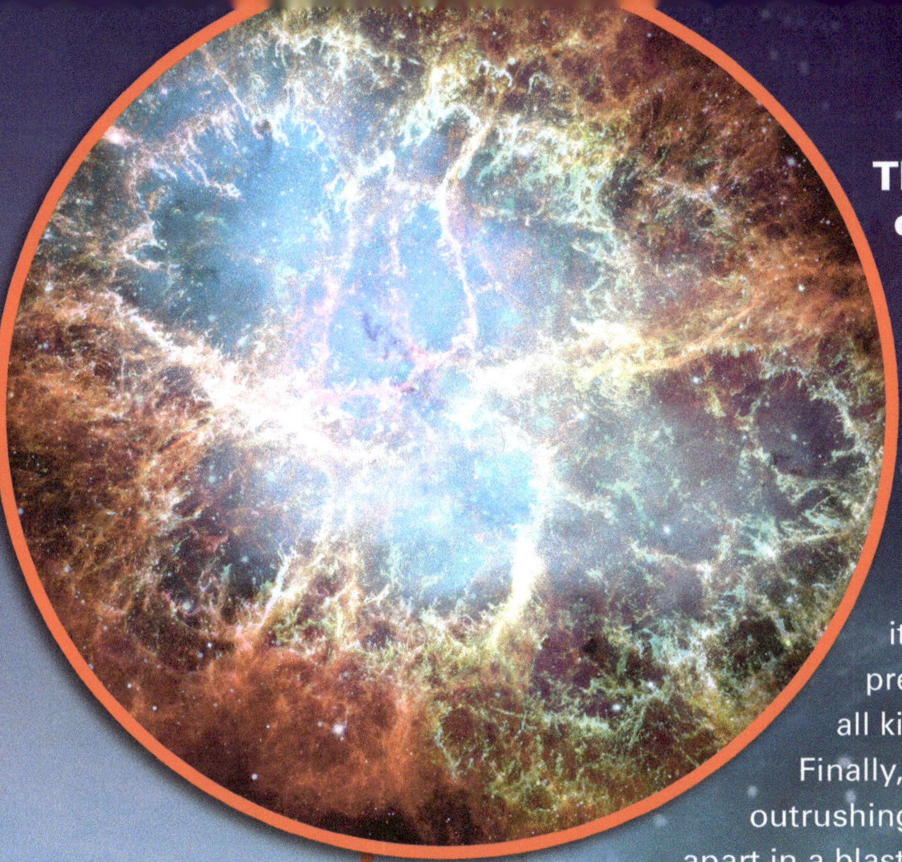

The largest stars continue to fuse heavier elements until they form iron. Fusing iron, however consumes more energy than it produces. A star that reaches this stage runs out of energy and collapses in on itself. As it does, the increasing pressure fuses the iron into all kinds of other elements. Finally, a cataclysmic wave of outrushing energy blows the star apart in a blast called a supernova.

DID YOU KNOW?

Do you like bling? Thank supernovas! Supernovas are the only place where many heavy elements, including silver and gold, are produced.

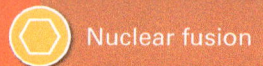
Nuclear fusion

Unlimited energy?

Nuclear fusion could be the perfect energy source. Fusion power can be made using hydrogen collected from water as fuel. Fusion releases harmless helium gas as a byproduct, not climate-altering carbon dioxide. It produces no harmful radiation or radioactive waste, unlike **nuclear fission**. Fusion can produce a constant flow of energy, unlike wind and solar power. What's not to love?

It's a long road, though. Because we can't achieve the prodigious pressures found at the cores of stars, we have to heat fuel to extreme temperatures instead—tens of millions of degrees! That requires high-powered lasers, which use up a lot of energy themselves. The trick is to make a fusion reaction efficient enough to be self-sustaining—that is, to produce more energy than it consumes.

Technologists have long dreamed of producing power that is too cheap to meter, as well as the transformative effect it would have on society. Could we harness the power of nuclear fusion?

The International Thermonuclear Experimental Reactor (ITER) will be the testbed for future nuclear fusion technology. ITER is being built in France with the help of 35 countries. The system confines plasma inside a tokamak, a toroidal (donut-shaped) compartment. It's like a fusion donut! Technologists are hoping that the first round of fusion power plants will be developed using the lessons learned at ITER. It's not all nuclear reactions and rainbows, however. The ITER program is billions of dollars over budget and decades behind schedule.

TECH TIME

The world has bet most of its chips on ITER for fusion. There are some side-bets, however. Many private companies are trying approaches other than ITER's titanic tokamak. Some use a technique called inertial confinement. In inertial confinement, a small fuel pellet is balanced inside a reaction chamber. Dozens of high-powered lasers heat the pellet to millions of degrees and—bang!—nuclear fusion occurs.

Visualizing half-life

What you'll need:

- 100 to 200 coins or other small objects with two distinct sides (coated candies can also work)
- Plastic bag
- Paper (graph paper makes it easier to prepare the half-life graph)
- Colored pencils or markers

Give it a try:

1. Place 100 coins in the bag and shake them up.
2. Carefully pour the coins onto a table.
3. Separate the coins that landed on heads from the coins that landed on tails. Write down how many coins landed on heads.
4. Put the coins that landed on tails into the bag and mix them up.
5. Repeat steps 2 through 4 until all the coins have landed on heads.
6. Now, make a graph of your data, with coins as the y-axis and number of flips as the x-axis. See the example on the right.

The chance that a particular radioactive isotope decays is like the flip of a coin. Here's a way to visualize how all those coin-flips add up to create a substance's half-life!

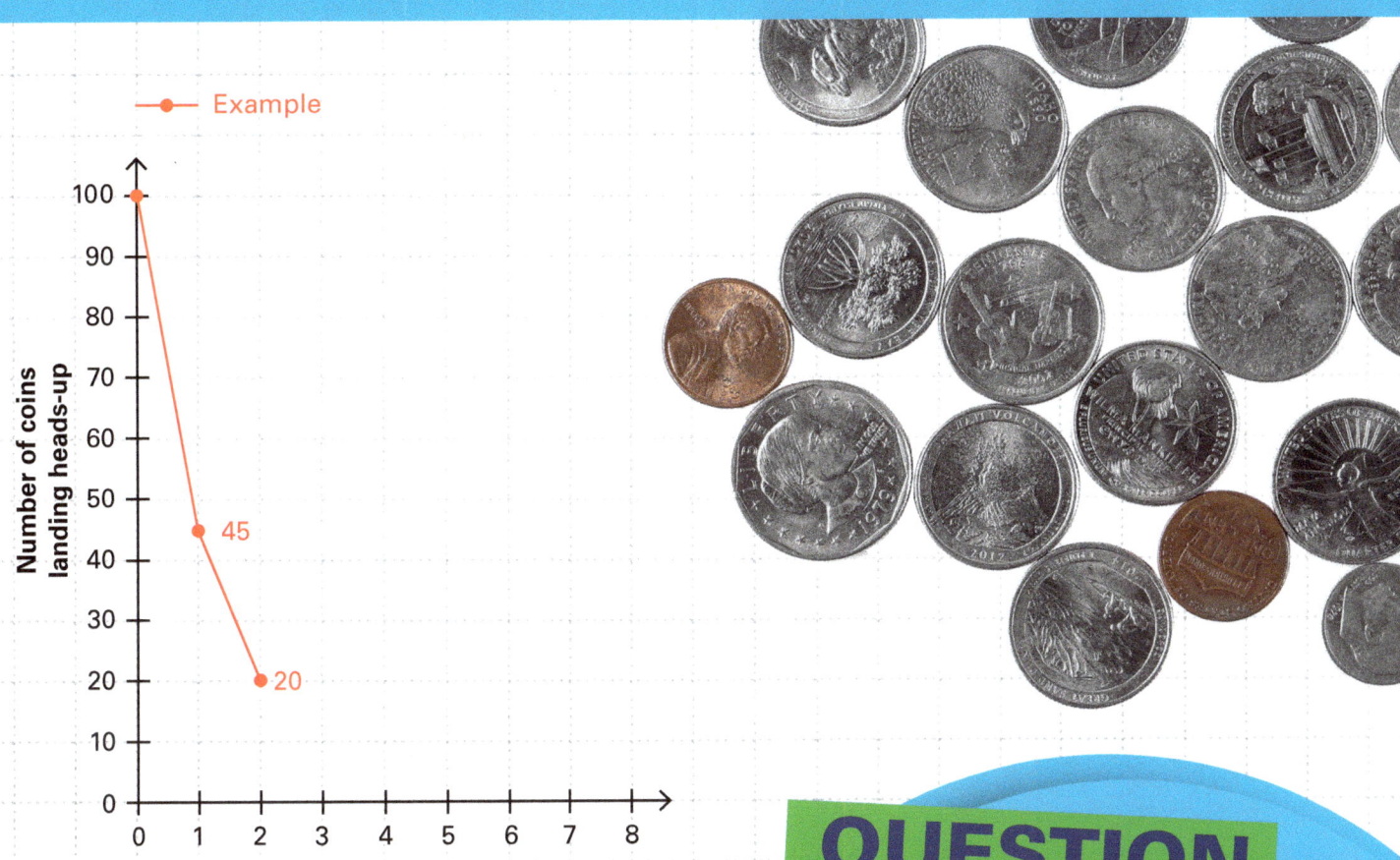

Try this next!

Repeat the experiment. Try using more and fewer coins. Record your results on the same graph in different colors. How do the results compare with the first experiment? Are they the same or different?

QUESTION TIME!

In this experiment, shaking the bag and pouring out the coins only took a few seconds each time. That's the half-life in our experiment. How long would it have taken for all 100 coins to flip to heads if the half-life was a day? A year? A thousand years?

Index

A
alpha decay, 26-28
americium, 28
archaeology, 29
atomic mass, 14-15, 22-23, 34
atomic number, 12, 22, 34
atomism (ancient Greek philosophy), 7

B
beta decay, 26-27

C
californium, 22-23
cancer, 30
carbon, 40
chain reactions, 32-33, 36-37
Chernobyl power plant, 39
criticality, 36
curium, 22

D
Democritus, 7

E
$e = mc^2$ (equation), 25
Einstein, Albert, 25
electromagnetic force, 18
electrons, 8-9, 12, 14, 26, 28
emergency exit lights, 29

G
gamma decay, 27, 35
gold, 41
granite, 35

H
half-life, 20-23, 29, 44-45
helium, 12, 22, 26, 28, 40, 42
hydrogen, 12, 40, 42

I
inertial confinement, 43
iron, 41
Island of Stability, 21
isotopes, 14-15, 20-21, 24, 27-29, 31-32, 35, 45
ITER (nuclear fusion experiment), 43

K
Klaproth, Martin H., 34

L
lasers, 42-43
lead, 12
Leucippus, 7

M
medical uses of radiation, 30-31, 35
Mendeleev, Dmitri, 11

46

N

neodymium, 15
neptunium, 20
neutrons, 8-9, 12, 14, 18, 21, 23, 26, 32-33, 36-37
nitrogen, 40
nuclear fission, 32-39
nuclear fuel, 36, 38, 42-43
nuclear fusion, 40-43
nuclear meltdowns, 38-39
nuclear reactors, 36, 38-39
nuclear waste, 38
nuclear weapons, 37, 39

O

Oganessian, Yuri, 19
oganesson, 19-20
oxygen, 9, 40

P

paleontology, 29
Péligot, Eugène, 34
periodic table, 10-13, 16, 19, 23
Perrier, Carlo, 17
pitchblende, 34
plasma, 43
positrons, 26
protons, 8-9, 12, 14, 18, 21, 26, 32

R

radiation shields, 35
radiation therapy, 30
radioactive decay, 14, 20, 24-32, 38, 45
radioisotope thermoelectric generators (RTG's), 31
radiometric dating, 29
radium, 27

S

Segre, Emilio, 17
silver, 41
smoke detectors, 28
space exploration, 31
stars, 40-41
strong nuclear force, 18
supercriticality, 37
supernovas, 41
synthetic elements, 16-24

T

technetium, 17
tokamak (nuclear fusion device), 43

U

ultraviolet light, 35
uranium, 32, 34-37
Uranus, 34

Glossary

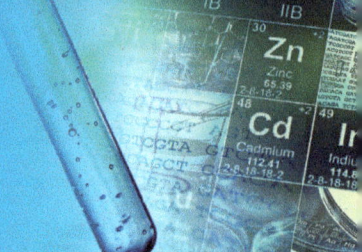

atomic mass (uh TOM ihk mas)—a measure of how heavy an isotope or element is. It is expressed as a number without a unit, representing the mass of an isotope or element relative to $\frac{1}{12}$ the mass of a carbon-12 atom.

atomic number (uh TOM ihk NUHM buhr)—the number of protons in the nucleus of an atom of a particular element. All atoms of the same element have the same atomic number, which determines the element's place in the periodic table.

criticality (KRIHT uh KAL uh tee)—the state in which a quantity of fissile material (material able to undergo nuclear fission) is large enough to sustain a nuclear chain reaction

electromagnetic force (ih LEHK troh mag NEHT ihk fohrs)—one of the four fundamental forces in physics. The electromagnetic force consists of two parts: the electric force and the magnetic force.

half-life (HAF LYF)—the length of time taken for half the atoms in a sample of a radioactive isotope to decay

isotope (EYE suh tohp)—one of two or more atoms of the same chemical element that differ in the amount of matter they contain. Isotopes of the same chemical element have different atomic masses.

nuclear fission (NOO klee uhr FIHSH uhn)—the splitting of the nucleus (core) of an atom into two nearly equal lighter nuclei

nuclear fusion (NOO klee uhr FYOO zhuhn)—the combining of two atomic nuclei to form the nucleus of a heavier element

radioactive decay (RAY dee oh AK tihv dih KAY)—the spontaneous disintegration of a radioactive substance, at the characteristic rate of the particular radioisotope, and accompanied by the emission of nuclear radiation

strong nuclear force (strawng NOO klee uhr fohrs)—the strongest of the four fundamental forces in physics. The strong nuclear force is responsible for holding the nucleus of an atom together, overcoming the mutual repulsion of the positively charged protons.

supercriticality (SOO puhr KRIHT uh KAL uh tee)—the state in which the amount of fissile material exceeds the critical mass required for a self-sustaining nuclear chain reaction. A supercritical mass can rapidly release large amounts of energy in the form of a nuclear explosion.

synthetic element (sihn THEHT ihk EHL uh muhnt)—an element that has been artificially created by scientists, rather than occurring naturally on Earth

www.ingramcontent.com/pod-product-compliance
Lightning Source LLC
Chambersburg PA
CBHW061255170426
43191CB00041B/2428